A reminder of
took place before you were born!

Many Happy Returns
Love,
Cousin John

30/11/2001

CENTRAL ENGLAND 2000

Edited by

Becki Mee

First published in Great Britain in 1999 by
POETRY NOW
Remus House,
Coltsfoot Drive,
Woodston,
Peterborough, PE2 9JX
Telephone (01733) 898101
Fax (01733) 313524

HB ISBN 0 75430 805 7
SB ISBN 0 75430 806 5

FOREWORD

Although we are a nation of poets we are accused of not reading poetry, or buying poetry books. After many years of listening to the incessant gripes of poetry publishers, I can only assume that the books they publish, in general, are books that most people do not want to read.

Poetry should not be obscure, introverted, and as cryptic as a crossword puzzle: it is the poet's duty to reach out and embrace the world.

The world owes the poet nothing and we should not be expected to dig and delve into a rambling discourse searching for some inner meaning.

The reason we write poetry (and almost all of us do) is because we want to communicate: an ideal; an idea; or a specific feeling. Poetry is as essential in communication, as a letter; a radio; a telephone, and the main criteria for selecting the poems in this anthology is very simple: they communicate.

CONTENTS

ODE TO MICHAEL HOROWITZ

I saw an old jazz poet last night
in a jaded venue in Leicester Square
he came to read some poems and sell some books.
Strange, then, that he could not remember his books
and could not see to read fluently from the page
and would not look us straight in the eye
for fear of recognising our concern

for a man of his age
we saw
an old man
blowing a kazoo in a nervous fashion
wearing a lilac cardigan
funny a few times but not enough
Animated only by words

A young and vigorously discerning crowd
applauded, sometimes honestly,
but with a sense of exasperation,
we could not help but wonder
whether the words were enough.

Fiona Louise Brice

WATERS OF CONTEMPLATION

The great enamel listener does beckon
As a child I loathed the call
And desperately tried to reason.
I pour another bourbon,
As I listen to the lucid waterfall.

Irony has it I now choose to lay
In the waters of contemplation.
Aye, I am no philosopher
Just a man who likes his say
whilst in daily lavation.

Outside these bricks, life struggles past.
I long for a peaceful atmosphere,
But within the raging oceans,
More wrecks are forecast.
Who will subdue the innocent fear?

Slowly and deeper I sink,
Cleansing body and tangled mind.
Can we escape the pain on the faces
Of humanity on the brink?
It's true pity can be blind.

The soap slides from my fatigued clench,
As life's last breath leaves another
Poor sod alone.
He couldn't stand hatred's stench.
Once somebody's dear brother.

I dry with much vigour,
To rid myself of today's news.
What good are my worries?
The world I am still in awe,
And waters of contemplation I will always choose.

Sherree Dudley

A NEW BEGINNING

The year 2000, a year of wonder,
what dreams, what magic
await us.

Hand in hand we take these steps
and marvel the beauty that surround us.

How wondrous this moment, this
magical moment, as we
enter this new world of
pure imagination

We are dreamers of a dream,
a wondrous dream of illumination,
a beginning so new, so true.

This is our moment, a new moment
in time we yearn for, what dreams,
what magic await us.

With hope in our hearts and dreams to
wish for, this is our moment, as
we walk hand in hand into
a new beginning.

Sho S C Tang

I Can't Yet . . .

I can't yet see
My eyes are still shut,
Closing out the world
Stopping me from seeing evil.

I can't yet feel
My hands are tight fists,
Holding in my fear and strength
Stopping me from feeling pain.

I can't yet taste
My mouth is still shut,
Holding in my speech and sound
Stopping me from saying how I feel.

I can't yet smell
My nose is not alive,
Holding back the smell of flowers
Stopping me from smelling life.

I can now hear
My ears, eyes, nose, mouth and hands are alive,
I can touch, hear, taste, smell and see
Thank you for giving me a chance.

Abortion would have scared me
Thank you for not killing me,
Love is a special bond I have with you
Thank you for giving me life.

Becki Stratton (14)

TRAPPED

I'm trapped in a place,
With no exit to see.
I'm not even sure,
If you can hear me.

I'm scared and I'm lonely,
I'm new to all this.
To be able to talk to you,
I sorely miss.

All I can see,
Are blurred shapes and light.
Distinguish you I just can't,
Try as I might.

My arms they feel,
As though they are tied.
Stuck forever,
To my unmoving side.

My legs feel as though,
Weighed down by lead.
Dear God how I wish
Sometimes I was dead.

If that driver hadn't drunk,
And got in his car.
I would now be normal
Just as you are.

R E J Bierton

JEREMIAD

Different faces come through the night
to take their seat under candlelight
from a million bright shining stars
pinks and greens, oranges and reds.
She loves to see it pleased
loves to see it worshipped
adored and adorned in fine silks and fabrics.

We gathered here to take precedence,
to choose our own fate,
and take power away from her fingertips.
The little beast she keeps at her heel
feeds it on chunks of peeled fruit.
Some would admire its beautiful simplicity
but the pragmatic find no joy in vain ideals.

Our queen begins the chant,
swaying a little in the night breeze
are voices join to sing the facets of being
as she raised up in crescendo
the glinting blade drawn swiftly from hiding
plunges deep, felling her in one
the blood lacing the black soil.

In shock we draw to recoil
the bodies becoming rock,
before the blade hits the earth
the testament of our own desire
hatred of such innocence
bares us to centuries of erosion
ring of stone binding us as one.

R Whiting

MEHEFIN

Instead of Burger King or Siop Y Prom
Try the floor of stones,
The plate tectonics large and small
Of coloured worlds that shape the sea.
White-scarred by quartz
This igneous bed of spots and stains
Bears seaweed strands,
Manannan's hair,
Wet and lustrous, flaming splayed and
Guarded by a gull,
As the trickling tide lifts his treasure,
Brings it in to where
A wig of weed and half a cod in batter
Nudge in a shallow pool.

And from the glassless terrace
A man treads as if still dreaming,
Stoned by his purpling veins,
Pyjama'd, tufted by his morning sleep
Yet generous to the children's stares
As his slippers take in water.

S Spedding

FAREWELL, SWEET SUMMER

There is a poignancy in the month of August,
Sweet summer has run her vibrant term of life,
Now autumn waits to pounce and drag her screaming
Down to his lair, and make of her his wife.

He will not tolerate her lush green foliage,
His envy makes her tone her colours down,
Makes her submit to his cruel code of fashion,
And dresses her in gold and russet gown.

Her brilliant dawns which once were pure and rosy,
Will sluggish start amid a veil of mist,
The apples burgeoning in the field and orchard,
Swell up with pride, their cheeks with scarlet kissed.

No more the skylark sings above her pastures,
The pregnant grain is raped with autumn's plough,
Her precious scent of flowers fades to oblivion,
Where will the bee's lips cull their nectar now?

Where once her footsteps trod the beach at leisure,
Now stalks a phantom grey - not so sedate,
The twinkling waves once sparkling and quite gentle,
Now slash the shore with violent crashing hate.

Summer's crown of life was starred with blossom,
Her meadows verdant, her skies an azure blue,
Autumn has stripped his bride and left her shivering,
She bows her head in shame - whispers adieu!

Summer's love affair with Spring is over,
The remnants of her love grown stale and old,
Do not rejoice at her fate cruel Autumn,
Winter's embrace is iron hard and cold!

Susan Edwards

THE DAY THE DARKNESS FELL

I stood upon the hill and looked out into the valley.
My erratic heart forewarned and feared of this the stricken alley.
I stood motionless both excited and afraid, as in the distance
I did see
A solid wall of darkness racing through the valley as if intent
on me.
Shrieks of nature filled the air in the blackened world
that spelt confusion.
While frenzied flights to who knows where, bore marks of natures
greatest intrusion.
Silence fell upon the world as it waited in the wings,
prepared for retribution,
While I took comfort in human knowledge and waited for the
inevitable solution . . .
Daylight

Floyd Coggins

PASSAGE OF TIME

My grandfather was born
in eighteen thirty-seven,
the year Victoria became queen,
a memorable date you will agree.
My father saw her, waved a flag
when she celebrated her Diamond Jubilee.

My grandfather died aged ninety-three.
I remember him, a small stiff man
whose gruff voice slightly frightened me
until the twinkle in his eye I'd see.

My father born in eighteen ninety-four
had hoped to outlive this century
but died, still wise and bright
at the age of one hundred and two
(not something many people do).

So, although I'm past three score and ten,
you'll understand it's my responsibility
to welcome in
the new Millennium.

Vivien Bayley

ON THE BRINK

Standing on the brink of time looking forward reflecting back,
For western world one man stood prime
To change calendar and history of mankind.
Hundreds and thousands of years before, swept aside as old folklore.

Pushing forward not looking back, destroying rain filling forests
                                                and meadows green.
'Til flora and fauna rarely seen.

Expectations, new inventions.
Technology increasing for some to have ease.
Time racing, nations pacing, material things to use, to please.
Ignore earth warning to take stock and fear.
Nations growing year by year,
Water valued more than gold.
Global warming, earth life sucked cold.

Pushing forward reach for the stars.
It is cold and ugly here on Mars.

Jane Darnell

ELEGY IN A WARM ROOM

Discreetly, echoes of the mind
slip back into neglected years to seek
the consolation of your image there.
Wave upon wave has flooded over it,
and at the outset I had pledged
it would not fade. It fades,
and to prevent its fading I am powerless.

The prison of the present walls me in,
and time forbids me time
to resurrect the past or spend
more than a passing moment to reflect on it.
For my humanity and lesser sins,
I am constrained to listen to
the siren call of more immediate things,
while only harmless echoes pass
infrequently outside its boundaries.

Michael Limmer

WHERE'S MEG?

Silence from the kitchen
Though supper's to be made
Feels like something's missing
And the table's still not laid

The Hoover's gathering dust
And there's dust upon the shelves
Knives tarnished with rust
Go blame it on yourselves

Grass in the garden
Growing taller by the day
A heart that had to harden
That simply couldn't stay

Born free to live a slave
Tied to domestic bliss
Bold, bright and finally brave
This life she won't miss

Like shackles made of iron
The ironing held her down
While inside she was dying
And couldn't hang around

So when you ask about her
And see her life as tough
There can only be one answer
 . . . Meg has had enough

K Smette

THE PARK AT BRETTON

Vistas of a breathtaking beauty -
bathed in a sun-drenched landscape -
where I sit spellbound.

Wind towers stand sentinel -
in elegant attitude -
against the azure sky.

Wander beneath beautiful trees -
towering towards the heavens -
an abundant arboretum.

Henry Moore's robust rounded forms -
stand solidly -
where grazing sheep shuffle contentedly.

A fantastic family of sculptural wonder -
bedeck a rise -
where Barbara Hepworth once strode.

From creation to contemporary -
from Rodin to Von Ridingsvard -
forever changing -
forever growing -
an eminently exciting place.

Pam Dawkins

SHAKESPEARE'S LAMENT

Hear it now and know how Britain the island of the mighty
Sold itself to slavery at the bidding of the Euro.
See how her men of old, heroes of cruel sea and bloody battlefield
Gave their wasted years and shed their wasted blood,
That we in contempt of their lives
Hand over piece by piece the sovereignty they died protecting.

Mark how our European neighbours in base jealousy
Have plotted throughout the ages as history declares
The overthrow of this sacred earth.
Whereas in past they failed by might, they now attempt
With stealth, soft words and fawning pleasantries
The subjugation of John Bull assuming, as they do
His fire's put out by the dawning of New Labour
Who lured us with the Utopia of the free market
Only to lead us instead in chains to the answering
Of our cousins France and Germany.

Think not however, the grass is greener across the water for it is not so
And note, we free men with a thousand years of self-determination
Now stand on the edge of our darkest abyss.
Where for want of courage the mire of federalism waits to swallow us.

But let it yet be shouted from the rooftops and declared
Aloud in every hamlet, village town and city,
In every inn and tavern in England that all is not yet lost.
If we can draw upon ourselves draw deep upon our very souls
And acknowledge all that makes us what we are,
If we can yet but find that thrice valiant, unending valour in our English
We may still turn aside this most insidious invasion,
Turn ourselves from the rack and ruin of the Bundesbank.
And stand as God always intended we should stand
In the face of universal corporation . . . free men, free men.

J Bingham

CENTURY'S END

The turn of another century is in sight.
So why is this one different? What marks it apart from all the others?
We have counted two thousand years but that is not a true date.
Man has existed much longer than that small span of time
And is little more than a child compared to the world's life.

But it is not the world's past that concerns us now.
It is our own as the end of the century draws closer.
Our past is bloody and filled with bad choices.
But we have changed, haven't we?
We have learnt from our mistakes, haven't we?
No!

We are still hell-bent on self-destruction.
It is in our nature and we cannot escape it.
Fate will do what it will with us, we cannot control it.
We deceive ourselves that we are masters of our own fate,
Free to choose our own path. It is self-deception.

The world moves fast towards centuries end, too fast for most of us.
Will the new century change anything for most of us? I doubt it.
The world will still go on, for better or for worse.
What does the millennium really mean?
Nothing!

Julie L Rickett

DAWN - LOCH MORLICH - 12TH AUGUST 1999

Beside Loch Morlich's still waters
Reflecting the heather's purple hue
I stood with you.

Mist clearing across piney tops,
The dawn so still,
As we two stood in awe
Before the majestic view.

Silently, so silently, we simply stood,
Both lost in private thoughts,
In prayers of thanks for all we knew.

Here, in the first light of dawn
We felt like we'd been reborn.
Each breath we took like Eden's first,
New, untouched.

Words were not needed,
For such would fail to fill
The feelings then we knew,
Instead a glance, a smile, a look,
Before a parting step we took.

There then, on Loch Morlich shores
We felt the breath of God,
And with grateful heart we sang,
Silently . . . still.

Paul T Walker

Us

(To Chris For Us: A Millennium
Would Never Be Enough).

Lover mine.
Soulmate child.
Mercurial angel.
Token sacrifice . . . as I.
Born in the blood of the Devil's moon.
Angers fuelled by the sensuality
of impassioned words.
You hurt . . . I know how deep you hurt.
Divinity now in the darkness of destiny.
Derivative of ecstasy.
The heart of you has always been
a part of me.
To say you are lover
Is not enough.
Falling unnoticed
A single Seraphim tear
For us.
Nothing and all.
Talon and touch.
Purest love.
Basest lust.
I am you.
You are me.
No longer alone.
No longer lost.
Anima . . . Animal . . . Animus
We are the one.
We are us.

Alene Kimm

MILLENNIUM

What does a dome have to do with it?
Not to mention viral infection
Of the electronic kind
We speak in terms familiar as of a next-door neighbour
And distracted, we look upon distortion
Priorities askew we fret
Caught in the realms of a 'what if . . . ?' mindset
We focus on that virgin time, around midnight's margin
When pumpkin pip will strike
Releasing a millennium as yet untouched
By war; by famine or disease
When oceans of pure unsullied hope
Will stretch out far and wide
But trapped, we live with imagery of dire events
To stain the night
And rain confusion upon dumbstruck soil
When in reality we hold the key
For whilst complacency is self-deceit
So fear, tinged with pale panic, becomes
Irrelevant
At odds with faith and all pre-emptive labour
Let us then gaze upon the reason for anticipation
On Him in whom all vestiges of truth lie bound
The One who longs to breathe, in each of us, new life
The very One who came to earth as man
And suffered here and died for us
If not for Him, The Christ
This measurement of time could not exist
But come He did
And this is His millennium

Kate Tavener

WORLD MENTAL HEALTH CARE

W orthy of government's considerations with expenses shared,
O utlawing negative thoughts blocking minds snared,
R ooted to outdated methods proved to be unsound,
L eading to disaster and despair all around,
D eliberate action is needed to stop decay.

M oney spent on world mental health care,
E ntices response from minds full of despair,
N oticing improvements they become more alert,
T rying to overcome bitterness and hurt,
A ll people suffering from mental stress,
L ose status amidst ignorance and thoughtlessness.

H eeding cries for help from the wilderness,
E nsures that psychiatrists should not guess,
A ll nations will then be aware,
L eading to a united understanding everywhere,
T hen peace may come to tormented minds,
H alting the flow of those left behind.

D eliverance from binding chains of mental instability,
A llows sufferers to move freely in our society,
Y es, everyone deserves a chance of happiness.

G Bateson

THREE CHILDREN DENIED THE MILLENNIUM

Lubbesthorpe, wearing his tin hat
And gas-mask, surrounded
By the bric-a-brac of war,
His framed portrait of Bomber Harris,
Incendiary fins and rusty shrapnel,
Toasted the lads of the
Luftwaffe, the US Air Force
And our own brave boys.
With his steaming mug of Oxo:
Give it to them hot,
Give it to them strong,
Give it to them every day
And all night long!
But Lubbesthorpe felt a disquiet.
His open bound volume
The Illustrated History of
The Great War, its grey photos
Showing plucky Serbs
And evil Austrians seemed
A bit of a puzzle
Lubbesthorpe mumbled
Inside his respirator.
It was all so confusing.
But he was glad when
The News said
Only three children
Had been killed in today's attacks.
Lubbesthorpe wondered about
That adverb *only!*

Peter Godfrey

POTSHERD

Its curve conveys
a greater arc; a pregnant bellying
of promise, a swelling
womb of clay.

A single curve of lip,
one side of mouth once dumb
turned by the imprint of a thumb
into a chip

of time, of history.
But still the hands that turned
this early mediaeval urn
remain a mystery.

Dylan Pugh

STUDENT NURSE

You lightly kissed him
And said, 'It will be alright.'
He clung to his rosary beads.

Snug in bed, miles away
From the chill of the mortuary,
You dreamed of his spirit
Dancing around your body . . .

Then out of your body
You flew to your demon lover,
Occultly loitering with intent
In a dark corner of the room.

You panicked,
Crashed back into your body
And cursed his name.

A final fling.

Roy Iliffe

ONE MOMENT

She looked up at me
I could clearly see
My hopes for our future together.

Her tiny fingers grasped one of mine
This moment would last forever.

Her first sweet smile
That seemed to say
We'll share this life, whatever.

Together forever never came
She was taken from me
Like a forfeit in some cruel game
Whatever will be, will be.

Jacquelyn Harby

THAT ROOM

It came again
Unwelcome; uninvited.
That same strange room
Like none I'd ever sighted.

Beamed and lofty
Desolate and empty.
Rotting floorboards,
Woodworm there a'plenty.

I climbed the stairs.
My heart beat fast.
What would I find?
The present? Future? Past?

I stepped inside.
That feeling I was lost.
Nightmares, for me,
Are much, much worse than ghosts.

Anne M Jones

MILLENNIUM FAMILY

He barbecues in sultry air
Then eats alone in plastic chair,
A chicken wing his paltry fare,
For this is the man of the millennium.

Across the town in pine bunk bed
His kids have bedtime stories read,
A kiss upon each troubled head,
For these are the children of the millennium.

With weary sigh she dims their light,
No adult fun for her tonight
With bills to pay and money tight,
For this is the woman of the millennium.

And next weekend he'll call at ten
And give the kids a treat, and then
All tearful bring them home again.
And on the step she'll greet, and say
'How are you?' and 'How was your day?'
Whilst willing him to walk away,
For this is the family of the millennium!

Julia Donaldson

JUNE MORNING

Waking as the light peeped through the open window, I heard the first
blackbird call to summon the feathered orchestra for the dawn chorus

I stood by the window and witnessed the birth of a new day

The sky was faintly streaked with long fingers of palest pink and a
warmer orange.

No stars had dared to linger to witness the miracle and
I was sure that no-one else was watching
the ever changing panoply of the sky.
This show was for my eyes only.

The wisps of clouds changed shape constantly, opening new vista's
and the birdsong swelled and a paean of joy rose like an anthem
to a new day.

I stood transfixed, with all my senses tuned to the beauty
I was seeing and hearing.

Then like an intruder in heaven, the clanking of bottles heralded
the coming of the milkman.

The spell was broken, and I went back to bed to sleep.

G R Bennett

OWL

When the moon is an ivory plectrum
strumming across the sky,
And the clouds are ghost ships
sailing hauntingly by;
Silently from out of an ink black night
emerges a shape that dips
and weaves,
A winged nocturnal hunter the darkness
of the night receives.

On the wings of stealth it rises,
Silent, into the deep black still;
Born to follow the creed of its kind,
Following nature's will.

And when the moon is an ivory plectrum
strumming across the sky,
And the clouds are ghost ships
sailing hauntingly by;
Silently from out of an ink black night,
when the wind breathes a mournful sigh,
Over the fields and hedgerows
a spectral shape will pass silently by.

Peter Morriss

RETRIBUTION

I feel your presence,
Hovering around me like a mist,
Droplets of ice,
The air of my cell gelid from your glacial breath.

I must make compensation,
You come to me to mete out justice,
My time of reckoning,
I must make redress for my blood-red crimes.

I am guilty,
Your demands for repayment must be met,
There is no absolution,
Hollow voices of victims cry out for retaliation.

I am afraid,
Trembling before the visitation of your dark revenge,
My acts bring their reward,
Final satisfaction for those I have wronged.

I see you now,
Bathed in awesome light,
Your black, black eyes,
Blades with which to rend my soul.

I cannot escape,
Come then Goddess and wreak your vengeance,
I bow my neck,
Take you sword, Nemesis, and end my suffering.

D James

The Hanging Forest

In the hanging forest voices of old cry sharp through a deadly calm,
Agonising screams of once corporeal mass still echo with
                                            recollectual harm.
The woods at once all come to life as daylight makes its final stand,
And as the moon lights up the sky loud voices holler throughout
                                            the land.

On bloodstained trees their branches weep and creek through
                                            marks of death,
And on where ropes upon once hung the wind blows soft with
                                            gentle breath.
For though Mother heals she cannot erase the past the forest holds,
And memories of lives now gone through methods evil vile and cold.

The hanging forest was once a witness to the most heinous of
                                            all crimes,
The senseless deaths of stolen mortals hidden from truth and
                                            forgotten times.
Through many an unspoken year the woods observed strong acts,
Of immolation to a malevolent force though time did obfuscate
                                            the facts.

The hanging forest began to die when the lives that entered did so do,
And with every soul that breathed its last so a tree would
                                            follow through.
Absorbing green to golden brown leaves fell from every tree,
Leaving the forest naked and bare a skeletal remain as far as could see.

Time cannot erase nor silence the phantom cries that fill the air,
Of man and woman, boy and girl slaughtered without remorse or care.
And so as years do come and go their disembodied souls haunt the land,
A present reminder that evil acts enforce a doomsday close at hand.

Mia-Joy

ANGELS OF DUNBLANE

A feeling of sheer sorrow and a huge amount of hate,
for the madman who walked through the Primary School gate.
He was a cold-blooded murderer who caused so much pain,
when he gunned down the innocent Angels of Dunblane.

No-one could have predicted what was to happen on that day,
As that twisted form of man took the innocent away,
Possessed by evil and clearly insane,
He bought devastation to the quiet town of Dunblane.

Sixteen tiny cherubs just starting out in life,
A daughter lost her mother, a husband lost his wife,
The teacher used herself to shield them from danger,
from the bullets from the guns that were brandished by a stranger.

What made him do it, what made him pull the trigger?
Did it make him feel mighty, did it make him feel bigger!
This needless waste of life, what did he have to gain?
Why did he take the loved ones from the people of Dunblane?

Did he have a meaning or a reason for this slaughter?
He took away brothers, sisters, sons and daughters,
I could never ever imagine the hurt of so much pain,
But I say a prayer and God Bless all the Angels of Dunblane.

Jane Smith

TRANSIT GLORIA

The wide naked eyes of a startled deer;
     The fleet furtive eyes of a rat;
The warm welcoming eyes of a friendly dog;
     The insolent stare of a cat.
The peep of a mouse and pink peek of a pig;
     The camel's imperious gaze;
The mischievous eyes of a cheeky young chimp;
     The tiger's venomous blaze.
The mini-brained eyes with their angry red rims
     In the small jerking head of a fowl;
The mad bad eyes of a charging goose;
     The be-spectacled eyes of an owl.
The irresolute doubt in the eyes of a foal;
     The quintessence of trust in a shire's;
The shifty side-glances of drink-sodden tramps;
     The cold glassy eyes of high-flyers.
The eye-catching eyes of a beautiful girl;
     The lecher's slits burning with lust;
The wonder-filled eyes of a wondering babe;
     The ancient's dim vision mid crust.

Millions on millions of eyes looking out.
     Each pair on a world of its own,
Conjuring up the fine wonder of sight
     From the beams on their sensing screens thrown.

But alas some blind bolt from the blue may descend
     To erase all life-forms from the scene
And to end this unique viewing moment in time
     For the Earth to roll on, all unseen.

J LeC Smith

CARNATIONS

Carnations, sweet scented, dainty blooms,
waits white-blossomed for the season's show.
A waste to pluck and place in rooms
where no bird sings nor wants to go.
Science guides the florist's trade,
no season's limit forms these flowers
nor wait for colourful parade.
There's now full beauty in mere hours,
tended and nourished by a spray,
flourish the whole years round and flaunt
dainty beauty bright in winter's grey,
their elusive fragrance lingers long to tease.
There is a price, a mortal one to pay,
these same flowers are tended by young children
in humid greenhouse many hours a day,
instead of picking blossoms in the wild.
The treatment brings carnations fast to bloom,
out of season, is harmful and brings dread.
Children toil in the shadow of their doom,
as blossoms throb in life the children now are dead.

D Jennings

SLEEPING DOG

I search your face at rest
You are astonishingly beautiful.
If you sleep the sleep of peace
Then I envy you
I do envy you.

Your repose is one of innocence
Mindful of that, should I re-evaluate?
I gain from you such pleasure
You are stability
And I, I am not.

Wake not into oblivion
It is no place for you to journey.
The days are solemn like winter
And I fear it
I do fear it.

When you expel a sigh
The warmth of your wavering breath
A visitation from summer.
Eulogising hope
I'd forgotten hope.

John C Kearney

THE BIG WARM DOG

Beneath the steep rust-smelling bank
The grass is dusty and reddened.
Lank summer nettles loll
To the sound of white water.
There is no breeze
Only the rising and falling
Of midges in the shade.
The river is old and powerful
As it laps against the beach of oval
Bloodshot quartz and flattened schist
Like salmon skins.

Out of the sun
The warm black dog daydreams
Of a world without insects.
His ears hunting for familiar sounds
Amongst the words of the man at the water's edge
Who stares at the float which never dips.
He never uses proper bait.
A worm maybe. Maybe not.
A fish if accidentally caught
Is swiftly killed on the dark red stone
Glinting with mica and scales.

As he stares at the water,
Coughs tug hard: taut fishing line
Hooked beneath the surface scars,
But the sun and time too slowly fade
The tattoos he never talks about
On both his arms
Except here, to the river
And the big warm dog.

B Toynton

RAM JAM

Lies the Ram Jam Inn
Still by the Great North Road?
As we sped by, my father would cry
'There it is - The Ram Jam Inn
What a funny name!'
But we never went in The Ram Jam Inn.
I wonder if it's still the same
Alongside the Great North Road -
That Inn that we never went in?
Me and Mum and Dad,
How I wish I had.

Was it now I wonder
Filled with Eastern splendour
Potted palms, beturbanned Indian boys,
And were the meals served silently
By those dusky handsome boys
Sons of Lascars or Sepoys
Those smiling Indian boys
In those halcyon days when we
Were so much more easily satisfied
And some small novelty like this
Was counted serendipity and bliss

But alas, we never went in
The Great North Road's Ram Jam Inn
And I can only guess what was within
How I wish we had - Me, and Mum, and Dad.

J V Archer

THE DARK HORSE

Gentle light that covers our soul,
Radiates around us like the moon covering the sun.
The beauty which follows cannot compare to your own.

From the dark, only light illuminates our eyes,
The fire within cannot be extinguished
No matter what we try.

A silent stallion dwells within me,
His colour as dark as night.
The horse's eyes, red as Saturn,
Is love just the same.

The dark horse breaks free of his chains
To journey across broken plains,
Stopping only to rest or take in the view.

Drinking from clear blue streams,
Fish darting past him like people in the street.
Slowly the stallion, dark horse, catches, mesmerises a fish
With his eyes,
He will not hurt it, but lets it continue on its way.
Soon the fish will find happiness,
Not with a dark horse, but with another fish,
Both as beautiful as each other in their own right.

The dark horse realises it's not meant to be,
And continues on his way.

Paul Shemwell

TIME

Time is something that slips away,
As we experience each new day,
It does exist but we can't see,
It's invisible but affects you and me,
How do we know if it's really there?
What is this time that we share?
Perhaps it's like a ghost, a spirit,
Not visible but we can sense it,
Powerful enough to change the world,
Making the young turn gradually old,
But cowardly enough to hide its face,
As it fills the unlived timeless space,
Sometimes it goes too fast or too slow
Either way it continues to flow,
So as each day we travel the track,
Don't forget that the clock can never turn back.

Catherine Barker (15)

PRAYER FOR EVA IRIS
FROM GREAT-GRANDMA IRIS

Along with my name -
　　　I give you my love
And a prayer that through life
　　　The dear Lord above,
Will guide you and guard you
　　　In His own special way
And grant you the gifts
　　　I wish you today.

May you always be loved
　　　And may you love in return
Soar high - a free spirit
　　　Be eager to learn
Find joy in laughter -
　　　A smiling face,
And grow like the Iris
　　　In beauty and grace.

Iris White

THE GUINEA PIG WHO SOLVED 'THE TIMES' CROSSWORD

His wrinkled, claw-like fingers, relics of a bygone fray,
Slowly turned the pages of 'The Times'.
Long ago, with his Spitfire in roaring climbs,
He soared up to the topmost skies,
To swoop upon Luftwaffe prey,
Like an eagle with sharp and deadly eyes -
A far cry from the single eye which now glittered in their place,
A shining solitaire in the lop-sided setting of his face.
For him there were no pleasant dreams,
Only nightmares repeating warning screams
Of 'Look out Red Two, they're on your tail!'
Heralding a lethal hail
Of thudding cannon shells,
Then searing flames and sickening smells
Of burning flesh and hideous pain,
Before bailing out to live again
As a McIndoe 'Guinea Pig', during agonising weeks
Of grafting bits of buttock to incinerated hands and cheeks.
He completed 'The Times' crossword with an enigmatic smile,
Felt a sudden weariness, closed his one eye for a while.
His pen fell to the floor with a silence-shattering clatter,
Far away he heard eight Brownings chatter
And a hundred Merlins hummed within his head.
His lion heart fluttered,
Then, like a worn-out engine, spluttered
To a halt and he was dead.
How very strange, Fate should decree
That 'Without them we would not be free'
Was the puzzle's final clue,
The answer being, of course, 'The Few'.

John Martin

BEFORE

As I look at the green fields rolling away,
All divided up by dense dark green hedgerows,
I wonder what went on in this place.
Maybe close-fought battles, without the smell of gunpowder,
Rabbits burrowing in chemical-free earth,
Men harvesting without a machine in sight.

A skyline devoid of any human presence,
Wild deer running free,
And trees, many, many more trees.

J P MacMurphy

GROW OLD GRACEFULLY

It seems to be law, an unwritten one,
that once you reach fifty, something has to be done.
All the clothes in your wardrobe are wrong, so they say,
Oh! You just can't wear that, throw it away!

You're middle-aged now, so lengthen those skirts,
Wear flat comfy shoes, nothing that hurts.
Stop bleaching your hair, just be natural and grey,
Who are you trying to kid anyway?

It's even suggested, 'Get rid of the car,
Take long healthy walks, much better by far.
You'll live so much longer, if you party less.'
Who gives this advice? I bet you can't guess!

It's not my children, they think I'm just fine,
In fact, they still tell me, I look thirty-nine!
Nor is it my husband, he still loves my 'mini'.
No! It's a neighbour in her full-length pinny.

She's over fifty, and boy, does she look it!
Someone gave her advice, and she obviously took it!
So listen dear Alma, you can laugh, you can titter.
I'm growing old frightfully, wearing bright purple glitter.

Pauline Jones

MILLENNIUM MUSE

The Future? What is it?
It's flown in a minute
Like a pretty soap bubble
that soars to the sky.
And it bursts in a second,
to make a child cry.
Don't ever try to hold it,
upreach your arms to enfold it -
- Close to your heart,
Future, surely, is Faith,
Courage and Love,
These Graces, to all, are
God's gifts from above.
Life is fulfilled with joys and sorrow
Here today, and gone tomorrow.
Time is a mystery
But we are in it
If only for a minute.

Joan Staniforth

CHANGES

The birds wake me up singing loudly
And suddenly mornings seem lighter
Before they were cold and so dreary
But now the sun shines so much brighter

The grass is so green and so vibrant
The sky is incredibly blue
This change isn't cos it's the summer
This change is because I've met you

The flowers smell sweet in the garden
There's a cool subtle breeze in the air
In the street my heart pounds with the traffic
Because I know you might be there

There's a bounce in my step when I walk now
There's a gleam in my eyes that is new
There's a feeling of anticipation
Just waiting to see what you'll do

In the silence of night I hear music
And I dream about holding you tight
I can vision your smile, hear your laughter
And I know that these feelings are right

Every day my love for you is growing
When you're not here it feels like forever
But I know that with time and with patience
We'll soon be in love and together.

Karen Horne

MAGICAL ENCOUNTERS

The mist clears over the evergreen wood
It sparkles with glorious light,
Sunbeams bounce beyond the hills
As the dawn replaces the night.

A gentle wind blows petals around
Where birds soar through the air,
And strong images of broken light
Passed over the morning so fair.

The presence of light unfolds a spirit
In a dream of warmth and desire,
Combined with nature's powerful strength
You feel the earth, the wind and fire.

Is this the time running out
Or has time already run?
The day draws to a close
As the night fades out the sun.

Helen Towner

As Their Freedom Flies

(It was not unusual to see gypsy caravans at
Chelveston Aerodrome in rural Northamptonshire
standing beside American *flying* fortress bombers!)
In old caravans china rattles.
Horses startled, snort
Silver bombers roar and snarl
into summer skies.
Gypsies look
and stare
as their freedom flies.

Paul Wilkins

A NEW YEAR

A new year is dawning
It really comes upon us
without any warning.
We are still in the year 1999
I'm sitting in my chair
with my usual glass of wine.
None of us knows what the future holds,
Let's hope at least it is free of colds
I'm still going to get out and about
as it makes me feel good,
If I could make everyone younger
and fitter, I would!
I wish all my friends and folk
I meet every day -
A warm greeting for the New Year
and good health . . .
            what more can I say?

Pamela Butler

THE MARK OF TIME

Time is like a tapestry
Embroidered with doubts and silken thread.
So uncertain the future appears to be.
Time can be precious like book much read
Words so unique from an author's mind.
Time is always moving on
Trickling away like sand we find.
Time makes a sapling grow strong
So stands one day a tree in bloom.
Time can rule men's lives
And go too soon.
Time hastens by like a swarm of bees in hives,
While the winds sow seeds on the earth
As seasons come and go
Awaiting rebirth.
Time measures in sunrise and sunset glow
Its long shadows cast.
Time is a memory we know
Cherished to recall the past.
Time can be empty like blank pages
That only a pen can fill.
Time is a leader of all ages
Helps nations unite at will.
Time is a wise counsellor too
On the answers we need.
Time is patience and questions few
But secrets are kept so deep.
Time rewards all who deserve the most
So here to Millennium when we raise
                    a champagne toast.

M Hanmer

THE SWALLOW

Sheltered from the wind and rain
where grubby hands must reach in vain
the swallow builds as summer nears
from mud and twigs a home appears

Snuggling warmly in their nest
the birds await an honoured guest
four tiny eggs alive and warm
they know will soon a family form

A gentle knocking from within
warns Mother that she must begin
to send her mate in search of food
providing for their little brood

Then Mother with a watchful eye
must teach them as they learn to fly
for soon will come the bitter snow
whilst from the north the cold winds blow

When once again these gallant bands
will soar away to distant lands
the reasons why I can't explain
for soon they'll all come home again.

John E Barnard

COLOURFUL TIME

We walk on ground with wild flowers.
The cold wind annoys my children;
Its whistling, rough playful antics
Moving every stem to and fro,
Many insects rock passively.
Silently we pass through, touched by
Leaves, flowers and soft grasses,
Avoiding the stinging nettles.
Tall thistles make the children cross
These delicate purple flowers
Encased in a guarded fortress
Jewels in a barbed-wire casing.
My daughter protests and stands still.
I carry her a short distance
Too heavy, stomach to stomach
My back and shoulders take the strain.
I stop, put her down carefully
We are at the end of the land
Sloping into moving waters.
I look on its glinting surface
Tiny insects bob up and down
As if worked by a puppeteer.
Over on the opposite bank
Separated fenced-in farmland.
Far into the misty distance
Bluey grey and reds of house bricks.
We focus on different things
I reflect on passing moments
And they on living today's time
My son on the 'giant castle'
With its flag violently flapping.
Am I losing him to his thoughts -
Future, ambition, direction.

My daughter concerned interrupts
'Do you know how many jam jars . . .?
I like the lemon curd fields.'
Today, motherhood is retainable.

M Rose

A NEW CHALLENGE

The seconds tick-tocking with relentless speed,
to our cry of 'Slow down!' They pay no heed.

The days they start, and as we turn around are over,
Leaving us still searching for that elusive four-leaf clover.

Days, weeks, months, *years,* fly by,
We look back, and for them only sigh.

Sunsets and sunrise with life's stories in-between,
'If onlys' and 'might-have-beens', in dreams are only seen.

With a new dawn soon arriving, hope will be intensified,
believing the 21st century will dry the tears we've cried.

But, it won't have a magic wand to make love paramount,
It is our efforts for love to reign that really count.

Jesus came amongst us on Earth to show us how,
to follow His example we have to do *right now.*

Alongside love, we know that peace comes close behind,
to stop the bombs and stem the blood, this is what we must find.

Countdown for 1st January 2000 is nearly begun,
It is looming so close on our horizon.

To repeat a mistake is the height of stupidity,
I pray *that* is not the future for humanity.

Joy R Gunstone

CHANGES

I made my entrance in this world
When gas lamps lit the street
And horses pulled the carts and traps
To markets, where we'd meet
The farmers and the traders
Veg, butter, lambs to sell
Our water didn't come from taps
But from the garden well
Grocery bought from little shops
From the baker we'd buy bread
Milk, in churns, delivered
Not bottled, jugs instead
Now progress through the passing years
Brought forth atomic ships
Television, phones and cars
And even microchips
The supermarkets sell all things
From clothes to bread and cheese
Exotic food shipped from abroad
To store in the deep freeze
But one thing that has changed not
Since this old world began
Are all the inhumane things
That man has done to man
Let's pray the year 2000
Will change the years to come
And the world becomes a place of peace
In the next millennium.

Helen Hyatt

A New Millennium Is Dawning

A new century is dawning, how will history be writ
Will it concentrate on politics or on the media's wit?
On single parent families, or life upon the dole
Political correctness or the Royal family's role

The advances of technology, the combustion motor car
The computers and the videos or how man has travelled far
From aeroplanes to rockets and a walk upon the moon
Or how the nineties pop stars could hardly sing in tune

Of wars and devastation and weather pattern change
Or the hole up in the ozone that will melt the ice again
Of increasing passions and violence on the street
Of tail backs on the motorways that widening roads can't meet

Advances in this century have been a giant step for man
But not everything is perfect, if you want to clone a man you can
Did people in the prior one know how far we'd come?
That children playing in their schools would be at danger from a gun

As we pass the year 2000 will these become the good old days?
Will we remember only good things and not improve our ways
The world must become concordant and then things will better be
We'll have to carry on with confidence and with hope we'll wait
and see

A new century is dawning, the nineteen hundreds will be done,
Will that magical two thousands bring with it joy and fun?
The millennium they call it yet it is just another year
But on this special New Year's Eve every eye will shed a tear

With the passing of this century every heart with hope will beat
That the shortcomings of yesteryear no nation will repeat
We must all go forward with longing and desire
That for peace in every country each mortal will aspire

We see a bright new future with this new century
The rapid paces of technology could mean our future would be free
No more wars or pestilence, no famine and no fear
But then we must remember this is but another year

Gill Brion

ICY BREEZE

Sometimes when I wake up
And from the window, I do take a look,
The frost-bitten trees
The icy breeze
The frozen bubbling brook.

The condensation trickles,
Down the windowpane
And forms a puddle
At the end of the frame.

A chill runs up my spine
A cold breeze enters the room,
Suddenly my day,
Is filled with sadness and gloom.

A moaning voice from not too far,
It's a neighbour 'trying'
To start her car.
The windscreens are frozen
The doors are still stuck,
Does not look like she is having much luck.

The dog's barking
He's been locked outside,
In his kennel he does hide.
A robin flies past
And lands on a tree,
Pruning himself for all to see.

Turning on the TV
The forecast does not look bright,
Looks like it's going to be
Another frosty night.

A Bastiani

PETER, THE ROCK

Sweetheart, lover, understanding spouse
Son and father, grandfather and friend
Gardener, carpenter, sportsman, painter
Mixing all abilities to make a perfect blend

Now I cannot touch or be caressed
An odd job man is needed for repairs
Nor can he hold me in the twilight hours
Yes, still I feel his loving and his care

And if I walk alone when it is dark
I feel more safe than when he was alive
For I am sure he guards me everywhere
When I'm alone, he's ever by my side

Dolly Harmer

CUMBRIA

When you travel up to Alston Moor,
It really is a scenic tour,
Such panoramic views abound,
To my eyes, it really did astound.

The hills, the mountains, fields and trees,
Like in a picture postcard squeeze,
A patchwork quilt of different greens,
Against the hilly background scenes.

We rented out a place to stay,
Called 'Kirkland' which we reached that day,
A bungalow of old world charm,
Set amongst such peace and calm.

The vista from the window square,
Shows rabbits playing, sometimes a hare,
From every angle sheep, sheep, sheep!
Chewing grass where're you peep.

So many places to pay call,
Carlisle Castle, Hadrian's Wall,
At Langwathby the ostrich far,
You can watch them hatch, away from harm.

Oh yes! this week has been exquisite!
With all the places we've been to visit,
As homeward bound, I'll rack my brain,
For when we can return again.

J Bright

Two Minutes Silence

It is when, the strong are weak
          the weak are strong
          the mighty are humble
          the humble are mighty
          the mightiest pay tribute
          and rulers obey
          the captive are free
          and the free are captive

It is when, the armless salute
          the legless stand
          the sightless see
          and mothers weep
          while we stand among poppies.

Jack Guthrie

NIGHT INTO DAY

A myriad of twinkling stars
Above your clouded head,
Sweet dewy grass beneath your feet
Where you do not dare to tread.

The babbling brook laughs at you
As it wends its weary way,
Stroking the fields it passes through
In its careless gentle play.

The full moon's shining light
Swallows up the darkened sky,
Creating shadows and illusions
That trick your mind and eye.

The soft wind whistles gently
In the calm still of the night,
Carrying the sweet scent of summer
On its never ending flight.

Night creatures stir to waking
Rising from their beds,
Now's their time to hunt and feed
Whilst others are at rest.

Soon the light is breaking
Stretching its arms across the sky,
Its fingertips are creeping silently
Pushing away the dark night.

Now the night is at its end
Another day has been born,
Spreading its light and warmth
As it does with each new dawn.

Jo Howson

SILENT FEET

Surrendering on silent feet to Sherwood's green embrace,
no sound I made, on mossy forest ride.
When, suddenly, the spirits of that lonely, leafy place
surrounded me, as if to be my guide.
They led me deeper still, despite my fears,
as each advancing step turned back the years.

They shepherded me gently back to medieval days
Their whispered voices echoed all around,
but of those spirits, nothing saw I through that golden haze
of paint splashed, dappled sunlight on the ground.
Was I mistaken? Was it just the breeze?
Or were there outlaw voices in the trees?

Their ghosts were all about me, as beneath the oaks I stood.
My fears were great, but greater still my trust
in this, my childhood hero . . . Was it really Robin Hood
there with his outlaws, long since gone to dust?
I, somehow feeling images unseen,
stood on the threshold of what once had been.

To emulate his daring deeds today, we must not try.
The modern outlaw cannot be allowed.
But in our hearts we must retain these memories, or they fly
away upon the wind, like summer cloud.
We must ensure the memory remains,
lest apathy turn future hopes to chains.

Roger Brougham

THE TREE

If I could only speak to you
If you could only hear
What tales I have to tell you
To fill your listening ear

I have seen birds mating - build their nests
Watched them feed their young
Seen their fledglings learn to fly
Listened to their song

Upon my trunk young lover's here
Have carved their names with pride
Beneath my boughs - in anguish
So many dreams have died

I have sheltered many travellers
Through storms and wind and sun
They take their rest beneath my boughs
When the day is done

How many summers have I have seen
Springtimes come and go
How many tints of autumn
Before the winter's snow

But now I have a message
I wish that you could hear
As man pollutes the planet
You should live in fear

But I am mute and you - alas
Cannot hear my plea
Would you listen if you could
To a message from a *tree?*

Lydia Barnett

REACH FOR YOUR DREAM

Reach for your dream.
In a place where God's presence is seen.
Among friends new and old.
Awaiting is the challenge for those who are bold.
In the beauty of God's creation
That will see us walking with determination.

Give thanks in everything.
Especially through the songs of worship we sing,
While reflecting in the Cairngorm scenery
Knowing that Faith has no boundary,
Offering us that extra step beyond
Where prayers speak and actions respond.

Reach for your dream.
Reach out and touch your dream.
Throughout your day to day living.
Search and the opportunity is always willing.
So don't be blinded by any blockades,
Where no dreams ever fade.

Alex 'Billy' Billington

FIRST DAY AT SCHOOL

Hands tightly clenched they make their way,
Attempting to be cheerful,
A new life starts upon this day,
Why do they feel so tearful?

A babe no more, to school they go,
The first time to be parted,
A sadness they should never know,
It's not for the faint-hearted.

Lips tightly pursed, no tears must flow,
As mum attempts false laughter,
The child must not see her feel low,
Her tears may come soon after.

A farewell hug, a smile, a kiss,
And care passed to another,
This dreaded day she'd like to miss,
Oh, who would be a mother?

John Sneath

CHANGES

Nowadays the world never seems to stop
You can even shop till you drop
24 hours a day you could just
Browse your life away.

Tills ding all night long
No more just the thrushes' song
Life doesn't shut down
Bustle and hustle, same as the day
Some use it to steer the blues away.

Motorways that once went quiet
Now flow along, all through the night
24 hour garages, more like shops
Not just for fuel, many others props.

Changes seem to alter our lives
Once I went to bed just after
'News at Ten'
Now at this time, I'm ready to go again.

Time will surely arise
When there will be no more, nine till five
Fast food hops, to serve you after your bop
Now they don't close at two
They bring in the early morning crew.

One thing will I think remain the same
That's the education game
Children will always arrive at nine
Because that's their time.

One good thing about all this
Old people won't have to sit and knit
They can do their shopping bit
No more sleeping pills, they can go and support the tills.

Pamela Blackburn

FIN DE XXIEME CIÈCLE -
A HUMAN COMPUTER MEMORY

A century full of disasters of human being crime
As to put in some jeopardy the whole of prime time.

A self full of empty void and nothing for sooth
Ever evading an eye for an eye and a truth for a truth.

A nation periodically sick with crass assassination
Then regrets and reflects; repeats after procrastination.

A country (now countries) of a uniform stalker on every street corner
With an eye in the shower head, say, an eerie ear in every sauna.

An uncle (long since) dying in his own single deathbed
I saw and remember, but never kissed nor so gratefully said . . .

A daughter ever striving to reach for the rafters
With nerves of fears and tears, never forgetting her laughters.

A son sent home superficially blood-splattered head to the toe
A step out of line? (zero-tolerance) despot benign? I've told you so.

A wife, a pure mother so loyal, so obstinate too, as not to be true
Never beaten, facially scarred, yet still not yet the black and the blue.

A mother, a father (mere et pere pair) never under one roof
So distant, so constant apart, as to appear somewhat aloof.

A cranium crammed full with www dot Internet and more
A heart and lost soul (camera shy, undeveloped) now head and
                                                    foot sore.

A poet amongst poets inferiority complex to shame and to blame
Yet all of our efforts of goals are but one and the same.

A princess (mag(g)i) I never married: as revealed in The Dream
Yet one got married in virtual reality - or so it would seem!

O' Immortal Imagination where th' eternal mosaic is seen
Breathtaking, Everlasting Majesty (glimpsed) so fit for a Queen!

A life jam-packed with I somewhat so call - intellectual ecstasy
From female form - so little seen! Still with so much of th' sex t' see!

A new millennium full of a bug; and a Cape of Good Hope
A new century still so clean; soon to be dirtied where there's only
soft soap.

P John Banks

YESTERDAY

I grew up amid back streets
Went to the corner shop
For a half penny worth of sweets.
Ran out of doors to scan the sky
To watch an aeroplane fly by,
Saw the lamplighter with his pole
Fed the horse that brought he coal.
Life was good, we had no telly
But Sunday tea was fruit and jelly.
Mum always there, she worked hard
A tub and mangle in the yard.
Stewpot in the oven, home-made bread
Money was short, but we were well fed.
My grandchildren talk of space
Life seems to be an endless race.
I marvel at the present day
But have we lost something
Along the way?

Rene Kowalski

YEAR 2000 - IN PUBLIC!

Now this is the year 2000! which we call 'the millennium'
The year most have been waiting to see,
On the tele, lots talked about it -
But I found nothing much to interest me;
    Then the Government decided to build something,
Much different! Something for all to see,
It was so big it covers acres of ground,
If in Retford . . . 'Why it would fill half the town!'
But no, it isn't in Retford, of that I am grateful to say,
But in London, the capital of England -
And it's there it's welcome to stay;
    They're hoping and praying for millions,
To flock into London, to part with their money and see,
This thing called The Dome,
But still . . . it does nothing for me,
Most of the cost, I'm sure it is lost,
In fact . . . you could say they have blown;
    On view there could be 'cheeky postcards'
The kind which we saw at Cleethorpes, whilst on a day trip -
Many years before . . . the last war,
They were published in Yorkshire . . . by Bamforths -
Famous for postcards along every seashore;
    Then there's 'The Kiss' . . . it's come back to Lewis
Of two lovers, carved out in stone . . . they're embracing.
Both being nude . .. in 1914 it was taken from view of the public,
For this, 'It is far too rude!'
Now this is the year 2000,
The year which all was waiting to see, but what do we see today?
Are lovers, 'they're making love in public'
    Whilst children . . . happily play.

Leslie F Dukes

HAPPY NEW YEAR!

There won't be time for 'doom and gloom'.
The seed is planted in the womb
and very soon this Mother Earth
will turn, and turning then give birth
to the millennium.

Some people give a frightened shrug
and whisper tales about the 'bug'.
I'll turn to them with my deaf ear
and raise my glass and drink a cheer
to the millennium.

Because surrounded I will be
by friends and all my family.
And we'll be drunk, as like as not.
We'll open bottles, drink the lot
to the millennium.

In years to come when people say
'And where were you upon that day?'
I'll answer 'Where I love to be
surrounded by my family
for the millennium.'

Glynis J Cooper

THE MILLENNIUM BUG

What can it be, it's puzzling me
This Millennium Bug, we can't see
It could cause such a lot of loss
And do we know who will be boss?

The Millennium Bug they do say
Will cause confusion every day
Everything will be in chaos
And do we know who will be boss?

The Millennium Bug, the millennium Bug
The Millennium Bug doesn't live in a rug
We don't know where to find it cos
We do not know who will be boss

M Topham

WHY DID YOU HURT ME SO?

Why you did, what you did, I will never know,
Why you put me through so much pain and hurt me so.
You obviously had your reasons,
But then I didn't know what they were.
Now since I found out,
The pain has been even harder to bear.
You sold me down the river
Knowing I couldn't even swim.
Only you and I know
You committed the cardinal sin.
You broke me, you destroyed me,
My spirit and my soul,
How was I ever going to fight back to reach
The unreachable goal?
But just like Humpty Dumpty who had a great fall,
I had to learn all over again to walk tall.
I found a handful of people to help put me back together again,
To help wipe out the misery, the suffering, the pain,
So I could get on with my life and start living again.

Pat Dring

PRAYERS FOR PEACE

How the world longed for a blessed peace!
Trying to bring it back more and more,
In spite of wars, strife and malice,
Enmity, disorder, hate and rancour!
Ah, the evils which preventing to gain
By peaceful few, to that glorious access!
Yet the efforts always meet disdain,
Corruption, wrong of lawlessness.
Please God, return to our broken hearts
Just but a part of glorious, peaceful years,
For we are struck by infernal darts
Praying endlessly to you with incessant tears.
Only You alone able all of us to succour;
Only You able to bring back peace and not distress;
Please dear Lord, banish from us strife and war,
And return to us back the joy of peace and happiness . . .

Stanislaw Paul Dabrowski-Oakland

SILENCE . . .

Silence is a stillness,
A moment's hush,
Silence can be stealthy,
Unreal, deadly.

Silence is a noise,
Stifled, muted,
Silence can be gentle,
Quiescent, tender.

Silence is a soundlessness,
An inaudibility,
Silence is a lull
In the midst of life's roar.

Silence is a gift,
A precious moment,
Given, to treasure
And explore.

Doreen Roys

TOGETHERNESS

If we were like sister and brother,
I'd see the care in your eyes,
but now we are lover and lover,
I feel it from deep in your sighs.

If we are like apple and orange,
we would lay side by side in the bowl,
two hearts that can search out and forage,
together our life is a whole.

To run hand in hand with each other,
would cater for all of our needs,
in union like father and mother,
the rest of our life sewing seeds.

It is always my wish to be with you,
to hold you and care for your heart,
giving all of my life with a love true,
thinking of you when we are apart.

D R Stringfellow

WELCOME TO THE COMPUTER AGE

I am house bound, nailed to the floor
Visitors won't wait till I open the door
Arthritic and useless what have I got
Besides a knee or two that's going to pot?

A brain that is not going to waste
I'm quite interactive in cyber space
I love conversation, e-mail is fine
I can't walk but I can talk, even on-line

Now I am learning to build a web-page
To talk to like minds regardless of age
My legs may not work but no need to fret
My computer and I are on Internet.

The world opens before me like never before
Canada and South Africa are only next door
Nineteen ninety-nine has opened my cage
Welcome to the New Year and the Computer Age.

Alma J Harris

SPRING SADNESS

Snow fell in the spring, that year.
The previous summer had been long and hot
And a pair of swallows had nested in the porch.
The had raised their brood and gone
And the winter had been hard and lonely.
It stopped snowing in that spring
The sky was grey and overcast.
Somehow, through the cold and damp
A single swallow made its way here.
It perched on my washing line
Preening itself and looking up into the grey sky.
For four days the swallow waited patiently,
Then the sun shone and it flew away.

Since that day, no swallows have nested here
And my porch is empty, white and bare
Every long summer.

R Cook

END OF AN ERA

Farewell to the twentieth century
Hello for a brand new start
Remember triumphs and tragedies
Long past, yet dear to your heart.

When man first walked on the moon
That time snow fell in June
Our Queen at her Coronation
The hype of super inflation.

We all have our own special memories
Of friends, loved ones now gone
And though, it's the end of an era
In our hearts, these memories live on.

The great wars, with our backs to the wall
Peace, when we all had a ball
Elvis, Beatles and the rest
The time men climbed Everest.

So many events and occasions
The likes we won't see again
Let's hope all future relations
Aren't filled with heartache or pain.

So farewell to the twentieth century
Good times, sad times now past
Let's hope for a brighter future
And try to learn from the past . . .

GIG

THOUGHTS OF THE MILLENNIUM

Earth turns on axis 24 hours a day
Spins around the sun to make up one year
Giving autumn, winter, spring and summer
This has been so for many an era.
What's all the fuss about this millennium?
Take a good look at the other planets
We're the only one with 'life' on it . . .
Have a good party, visit the Dome
And just be thankful you're still here.
The present is for children to enjoy to the full
Youth holds the key for whatever's to come
Those that have lived their lives up-to-date
Can look back and smile and probably say:
      'I did my best' . . .
There's little more I can say
Earth still turns on axis 24 hours a day
Continues full circle around the sun
Whether tomorrow is 2000, 1, 2, or 3
Mankind cannot change eternity!

M L Hensman

BEST FRIENDS FOREVER

Few people we meet are kind and sincere
Best friends for ever we grow closer each year,
You ask for nothing, you say you have all you need
Warm and loving you are indeed,

Kind and caring to all that you know
Wherever you are, wherever you go,
You give so much pleasure doing others no wrong,
May the path of life be both healthy and long,

A time to say thank you for all that you do
It's a privilege to be friends with someone like you.

C Gardner

AS SUNLIGHT STRIKES, A SMILE IGNITES . . . A SOUL!

The day strikes my gaze with blazing fire
A heartfelt desire, unknown
An almost alien inspiration captures my soul
The sunbeams seep through the green trees
From a distance, arriving to accomplish a purpose
Almost defining a particular field of intense energy
Ultimately, illuminate pure features of calm
In an instant, a sudden striking sunlight hits my face,
It smashes straight through my
Seemingly transparent veins.

In this contemplation of superb silence
I am enveloped by entire kindness,
As deep into the distance, edging closer up to me
I can see an image approaching,
As I sink further toward its connection to me
I reach out to embrace it in an extreme of anxious need
A desire to create it brings me amidst an unfounded belief
A belief meant to be . . .rising . . . finding . . .
Me! - for you . . . You! - for me.
Entirely.

Bharti Ralhan

THE WINDMILL

The windmill turned with ease and grace,
A slight wind blew across my face,
The fields alight with golden wheat,
Would call my childish running feet.

The windmill turned with oh such charm,
My love and I walked arm in arm,
The blue sky singing our own song,
Our happy hearts would jog along.

The windmill turns as now we stand,
Our children clinging to each hand,
Their eyes aglow, our joys abound,
We watch the windmill turning round.

I A Hardy

MELTON'S TREES

Green leaves adorned the tops
Of trees in spinney, wood and copse
Wherever Melton Borough reaches;
Ash trees and oaks, willows and beeches,
Turned their tresses to the sky
As Summer's smiling days strolled by.

But now Autumn's nights begin to freeze
The cool green tops of Melton's trees,
They change to brown, and red, and gold;
And as more icy, keen, and cold
The Autumn's winds begin to blow,
Those leaves fall to the ground below.

They spread an apron on Earth's lap
Beneath which roots can take a nap . . .
Then wake again, refreshed, revived,
When Winter's gone - when Springtime has arrived
To dress our trees in green once more,
As she has done so many times before!

Dan Pugh

KIDS

You feed them, change them,
Keep them warm, safe from harm,
Take their crap and their cheek
And retorts.
Encourage them, teach them
Bind their sores, fight their wars
Protect and defend them
And deny bad reports.
Pay their way, fill their day,
Make their path, take their wrath,
And just smile.
Listen and pray, watch they're safe every day,
Tread their path with them, sponsor each mile,
Give them dough, greet their mates,
Wait up on their dates,
Worry and chew yourself raw.
Miss them when they're away
Watch them go every day
When they're back you'll be there at the door.
Put their food on a plate, as they truck out the gate
Lie awake toss 'n' turn say 'you'll never learn.'
Give birth again each time they're late!
Wipe their tears, alay their fears for about
Thirty years then find out that it's
You that they hate!

Maxine Gardner

BACK TO THE FUTURE!

I can imagine the future
As I wait for my 49 bus.
No more blockage of traffic,
There's a spaceship, without any fuss.

Aboard was a robot for tickets;
No friendly face, or 'How do;'
We pushed a red light to get off,
And a green, if you want to go through!

Janet Brown

WISDOM

When I was a boy
I knew a man
Who was very old
But taught me to understand
The beauty of Nature,
Of doing most things right.
And helping the unfortunate
With all my strength and might.
Don't seek reward
My revered friend would say,
You'll get abuse as well as thanks
But keep on doing it your way.
I've followed his advice
For many years since then
And now I am a man
Who tries to be a friend,
A man of wisdom like he was,
To help the young ones see
There is no certain path of life
But accept whatever may be.
Wisdom is a blessing
Given to everyone
But not all tend to use it,
If they don't it's soon gone.

Raymond Kirby

THE DYING YEARS

Memories are brought back
Looking back thro' the years
Famous nights, famous names
The old records, new achievements
New events that occurred during the years
That have been passed suddenly on
The first Catholic President of the USA
Assassinated by a bullet
While people with flags streaming
Greeted their President,
Scandal in the USA Watergate
And recently the shady Bill Clinton
Brought disgrace to himself and family
The Kennedy curse continues, JFK's son
Killed in an disaster.
John Lennon assassinated.
Those sorrows should be shelved
And better revelations remembered
Invention of the skies fastest bird 'Concorde'
Sailing round the world solo, and the air balloons
Bob through the air
The computer age, then the world of sport
Bringing fame to Stephen Hendry, Steve Davis
And of course the other sports people who made history
Lotto was created, millionaires blossomed
Not forgetting the death of Diana, Edward's wedding
So many things to be recorded
When the new millennium does proceed.

Wallso

ONE OF THE MANY UNKNOWN SOLDIERS

RIP Dad and all world war soldiers, brave men in W W One, mustard gas, fumes, blinded, wounded, should read some of the true cases, were they lions led by donkeys?

In 1904 as a young lad,
Yes you've guessed I was my Dad,
The honest truths no lie,
A Scottish regiment the HLI (Highland Light Infantry)
In 1907 to India did go,
World War 1914 to fight the foe,
In the trench and left for dead,
Shrapnel bleeding wound in his head,
Taken POW by the Germans,
5 years underfed suffering by their hands,
5 children lost our Mother in schooldays,
Dad had to be both in many ways,
He prayed a lot - it was in vain,
For he suffered lots of pain,
His many grandchildren he did not see,
He never reached age as OAP.
ARP in World War Two as well,
Now this country gone to hell,
Looking down you see sign,
Form sign, form sign.
It's free country they used to say,
He was the best,
Now at rest.

Them that said it have passed away,
Signing forms and charity is a must,
European folks better off than us,
With plenty of things and food on the table,
Us British Council Tax Rate if able.
The gas, electric, water, insurance,
Mortgage and TV.

Us pensioners get nothing free,
A hearing aid, meals on wheels,
Us proud British greet deal,
Cousin's in families went away,
Australia, Canada and the USA,
Forty years and good job too,
Only one form to sign now true,
I wonder why I didn't go,
The state I am now you never know.
OAP proud son of POW W W One.

Scotch Tommy

SOLITUDE

Have you not been in the country?
Listened to the silence of the night,
When nothing has stirred the air?

Not even a butterflies
Transparent wings is heard.

Did this not make you feel
Nearer to God?

Jesus wanted solitude and peace
Time with God.

Like we too,
Need this at times
Yes time to assess ourselves.

To think and pray
For God to guide
Us, in all our
Ways.

Gladys Davenport

WALK WITH ME

Do not sorrow for me with leaden heart,
For I will walk with you.
I am the patter of rain, sun's rays, cold snow
The every changing world we know.

I am the gladness and the sadness that we share,
Understanding care.
A sigh that inexplicably escapes unheard,
A softly spoken word.

I am that morning chorus and rays of light
Just out of sight.
For I will walk with you, I shall not go
And you will know.

Keep safe a special key but turn memories away from me,
Unlock mind's eye and see
I have existed, therefore I exist too
For I will always walk in you.

S A Alcraft

IS BRITAIN THE BEST?

We talk of Britain with all our pride,
We've fought as Britain where many have died.

Over the years on land we have tread,
And on nature's gifts we have fed.

We've had lots of disasters in the air and on sea,
And we've never really had anything for free.

Royal and political scandals we've had,
The death of a great princess, that was very sad.

Each decade has brought a brand new trend,
So lifestyles have had to amend.

Music has changed in so many a way,
It's hard to keep up with the new trends each day.

At the end of the day when all said and done,
We want a world that's full of fun.

So you see it doesn't really matter where you live,
It's all up to you and what you can give.

There are always changes wherever you are,
Whether it be near or afar.

So you see it's not just Britain that is best,
But I have to say that we are as good as the rest.

Michaela W Garlick

NO STRANGER TO BEAUTY

We sat side by side on the hillside
watching the crystal white of day
slowly turn to yellow.
Each sun bleached horizon
merging with the next;
rows of lofty trees
marching in graceful disarray.

The sunlight caught the trees
where we sat,
brushing the top most branches
with pale gold.
Dragonflies danced around our heads
like fairies in some childhood dream:
light and beauty orchestrated
by a nearby tinkling stream.

Such was the pleasure
of simply breathing
in this aromatic trace,
I had forgotten that we were strangers
sharing intimacy and space;
each lost in that moment,
each found in that place.

Anne Palmer

THE MILLENNIUM

Time is a pocket watch in a Dali painting
Its solidity lost, it is folded and hanging
Over furniture. Time is clocks and chimes
And hour glasses, the poet's rhythms and rhymes,
The music of the heart beat and the metronome.
Mans earlier edifices will outlast the Dome.
Obeying the phases of the moon
The tidal wave falls on the sand dune.
The dawn chorus is an aubade to the rising sun.
Life is an allotted span, a race to run,
A wink, a blink, a twinkling of an eye,
A time to be born and a time to die.
Flustered by false calendars, doubting the gnomon's shadow
We plan to celebrate a birth date we do not know.
Like the White Rabbit preoccupied with punctuality
We count each fraction of a second to it with accuracy.
God's light will reward the focused attention of humanity.
A thousand years is a footstep to eternity.

Vivienne Brocklehurst

MY VERY BEST FRIEND

However I'm feeling - happy or sad, high or low
My teddy is cuddly and my very best friend,
He does not mind what I do or where I go
He is always there to comfort me, heartaches to mend,
Snuggling close at bedtime makes me feel secure,
Knowing he's on my side makes me strong,
Wherever I leave him I know for sure
I can always be myself. With him I truly belong.

I fretted missing him when away for the day,
Zoo animals are cute but not as much as him.
I wondered how he felt, what would he say?
Would he believe I'd dumped him? Chucked him in?
Returning that night I nervously clicked on the light,
Unable to face poor ted, filling me with alarm
Fearing he'd be grumpy and want to fight,
As usual he welcomed with a smile, my fears to disarm.

Kevin E Sims

MARTIN ASTLE

Though the empty church the notes
Drifted; plaintive, aching-sweet,
The last lament of a love-crossed swain,
Before he walked on dragging feet

To the long abandoned mill
To end his life's poor, shattered dream:
There with a knotted rope for aid
He hanged himself from time-worn beam.

Yet still it's said, on certain nights
The silent, star-lit air is rent
By organ music, soft and sweet,
As Martin plays his last lament.

And those who chance to stray into
The lonely lane that runs beside
The churchyard's creaking gate, may see
A silent figure softly glide

To where the mill stands gaunt and drear,
As once more Martin makes his way
To keep his rendevous with death,
As he did in a distant day.

P Wykes

ONE OF THOSE DAYS

Why is it when the chores are done
And everything is spick and span
I long to see a friendly face
Yet no one ventures near my place
No one calls on the telephone
My handiwork I view alone
I sigh and to myself say 'Deary Me'
I think I've earned a cup of tea!

But when the kitchen floor is wet
In walks Felix my darling pet
He leaves a trail of muddy paws
Right across my nice clean floor
The Hoover's going on the blink
And pots are piled up in the sink
The doorbell rings - well wouldn't you guess
Folk only call when I'm in a mess
Quickly to the door I hurry
To find the milkman wants his money
Back to the jobs that still need tending
Windows to clean and socks needing mending
There's a knock at the door - now who can that be?
It's the postman with a parcel for me.

I try once more but all in vain
There's someone at the door again
This time a familiar face I see
Come in my friend, have a cup of tea
There's no more work today for me
I've tried all day my home to fettle
So now I'll relax and let the dust settle.

Barbara E Rowly-Blake

IRIS

I didn't like you very much
As a child Iris
You were somehow unwieldy
I had no time for you
But now that isn't true.
Your stubbornness I can even tolerate.

I miss your dress
The bold colours
Of blue, mauve and yellows
Found in your head-dress.

I feel your curves
In different directions
Which seemed so unmoving
And never ending.

You are considered old fashioned now
And too big
But I like you more and more
I love you Iris
And would like to see more of you.

Though you are not around so much
I still see you in the park
Inevitably like so many things
There are changes all about.

But Iris you are still
My hardy perennial
And I hope this will remain so
I have fond memories of you.
Don't ever go away completely will you?

M L Vinning

LIFE ON THE STREET

'Any spare change' you hear my cry
You take a good look then walk on by
I am homeless, living on the street.
Any spare change for something to eat.
You look at me in disgust and horror
As though I enjoy to beg and borrow
If I had a choice I'd be like you
With a home, a family, a job to do
I'd give anything to go, to a shop and buy
Clothes and shoes that catch my eye.
Material things don't matter on the street
It's a struggle to live and find things to eat,
To keep warm in the wind, the snow and the rain
On Birthdays and Christmas to hide the pain
To find a doorway to sleep in the warm
As I lay down and pray, I see a new dawn.
Any spare change, you hear me cry
Please look in your heart before you walk on by.

M Dobson

NEW MILLENNIUM

A great new start.
A brand new day.
A time for us to change
In every way.

A new beginning
For us to share.
A new chance for us
To show we really care.

A time to befriend
Your fellow man,
And give them
A help in hand, if you can.

No more suffering
And no more pain.
Let the sun shine
Through the rain.

Bright new days
Are what we need.
We must say goodbye
To selfishness and greed.

Try to make this world
A better place.
By putting a smile
On someone else's face.

Christine Beeston

A New Beginning

Hail the new millennium
The old century passes by,
As we toast a new beginning
So many memories never die.
To approach it with excitement
World-wide the land will glow,
As we celebrate together
Our hopes will clearly show.

Hail the new millennium
Technology to the fore,
Sense so fast declining
Can speed increase much more?
Remembering man's achievements
Supersonic we must fly,
Oh yes man walked upon the moon
Unbelievable we sigh.

Hail the new millennium
We just hope and yes we pray,
Nature's love will still surround us
At the ending of each day.
As we face so many changes
The natural world must still survive,
Surely is the best incentive
For keeping everyone alive.

Dorothy Gillway

WHO

Has love displayed - no judgement made
With eyes so brown that never frown?

Who questions never, but loves forever;
Loyalty undying - no chance of ever lying?

When you need cheer, who's ever near;
Sustains with joy - and ne'er a ploy?

Who, left alone, has ne'er a moan
But when you come, to you will run?

What more to ask - in love to bask;
Who returns it all, when once you call?

Who - if you need - gives a love indeed
And won't abuse - who shall you choose

To love you well - come heaven or hell
And who'll love you, your whole life through?

A man you say? Oh no! No way!
Your dogs, of course!

Faith Legh

DAISY-CROWN DAYS

Can I go back to my daisy-crown days?
Perhaps there's a chance if I try.
Lie back in my chair, close my eyes and I'm there,
Where starry white fields meet the sky.

Please understand, I'm not scratching the chair -
I'm picking the daisies you see!
Maybe it seems, they are just in my dreams,
But they're perfectly real to me.

Stop holding my hand and talking so much,
Whatever is said you will find
I'm not home today, but flown far away.
And no one can follow my mind.

Yes, I've gone back to my daisy-crown days,
Threading flowers all day in the sun.
When it goes down, I will put on my crown
And come back to show everyone.

Audrey Bate

DOCTOR DOCTOR

Doctor, doctor, tell us true,
Because we don't know what to do.
Have we only months to live?
That's our life you're playing with.
Your time is precious we all know,
As on your rounds you cheerfully go.

Dishing out the pills and potions
Telling nurse to rub on lotions
Prodding here, squeezing there
Giving our feelings, little care.
Jabbing needles, x-rays, shaking head,
While we lie quaking on the bed.

Now you have got us in a lather,
When at bed foot you have a blather
Then smiling say, 'Can do no more here
You can go home tomorrow dear.'
Does that mean that we are cured
Or should we check that we're insured?

G W Bailey

REUNION DAY

Across the seas and through the skies,
Along the motorways and lanes,
Down the years midst joys and sorrows,
We meet each other once again.
Decades of years fall quickly away,
Endless nostalgia in full flow,
Squeals of pent up surprise and joy
Escape with love from hearts aglow.

Voices rise in pitch and applause,
Laughter breaks out with loud acclaim,
Hair styles reflect wisdom and age,
Though girlhood smiles are much the same.
School song links the years between us,
As we mingle in the village hall,
Cameras click to snap forever,
Present moments dear to recall.

High hopes were the aim of the day,
Two way tracks became one main line,
As past events were remembered again,
And school happiness came to mind.
Now in the years of age and grace,
Among the landmarks on life's way,
Memories of girlhood friendship shared
Are treasured in a memory bouquet.

Sister Gregory

JANUARY MORNING

O the soft pillow and the clinging warmth,
Fighting the strident tones of time -
Seven am and the morning, crisp
as a starched collar, gleams
through patterned panes of frost
as the cloak of night, gathering
a glittering hem of dawn jewels
sweeps to the West.

The battle won and misty breath
quickens as the morning toil begins -
fumbling stiff fingers light the fire
and vainly play before the cold blue flames -
The bathroom filled with steam cosily
deceives the tortured senses, whilst
the kettle singing merrily from the kitchen
melts the frozen heart.

The world is saner than it was an hour ago
as breakfasts sharp retorts
spit from the frying pan -
Another day begins with Winter's majesty supreme
and Summer seeming far away long the year -
The blustering wind greets the open door and
fractured clouds spill their bounty to
The January morning.

Derek Dodds

Man's Interminable Quest Called Progress
Cloning, GM Foods And The Like 1999

Guarded effusion from mortal lords
That cast their dirge across the land
Opening the door for new ambition
To come and rock once more
The ever changing force of life
But counting for nought in the ultimate
scheme of things
When all wiped out with a single blow

But purged from evil and like the
'Phoenix' rises from the ashes
Man, a mere metamorphosis of bygone life,
But never-ending carrying on.

Doris Hoole

MAP OF LIFE

Your map of life is open and spread before you,
Your longitude and latitude lines are drawn,
The compass is placed at the centre,
Now, which direction will you take, are you torn -
Between direction that measures success in possessions,
A pathway that leads into the world,
Or a heavenly form of ascension
That lets you live as your beliefs come unfurled.

We're brought onto this Earth without knowledge,
But our lives have innumerable choices ahead.
Our decided route of travel is partly our own
And partly in a direction we're led -
By a greater force who has gently pointed,
A way between *His* plan and your lives choice,
He who always lets you express your own thoughts
He who has given you voice.

Your map of life was an atlas,
A book of varying routes to your God,
With hills, valleys, oceans and mountains,
A trail that forever you'll happily plod.
Keep your beliefs on that pathway,
To feel His love always around,
From up in the heavens with angels,
To humanity here on the ground.

Valerie Wilhelm

A Treasure Lost, A Treasure Found

To us, it is a treasure lost
To her, a treasure found
For in the arms of God she lies
And not beneath the ground

Peaceful, she seems to sleep
Her face a silent symbol
That all with her is well
Yet we all seem to weep

For grief fills our hearts, as we know
Her smiling face we'll see no more
But memories of her fall before us
That we may cry no more

So as we're gathered here today
Let those memories, forever stay
And for our own selves let us pray
That we may meet with her one day!

Jassette Thompson

I Dreamed a Dream

I dreamed a dream of Ireland
'Twas a beauty I'd ne'er seen before
Of the beautiful lakes and mountains
And the wondrous cliffs of Moher
I dreamed a dream of Ireland
'Twas a magic beyond belief
The birds on high whistled in the sky
And you could hear the ripples of water beneath
I dreamed a dream of Ireland
Its people so lovely and fair
Then I opened my eyes in wonder
It wasn't a dream, I was there.

J McAdam

INNOCENCE

I asked of a young child,
Of that which brought happiness and
                              joy to her mind,
She spoke not of money or greed,
Or of that which those older, would
                              choose to find.

The love of a mother,
Who provided a home, where she could
                              find comfort and peace,
Of her friends, who shared their company,
Without ever the need of saying 'Thank you'
                              or 'Please.'

The innocence of childhood virtue,
Was still held firmly in her hands,
Sharing along with the years of youth,
That which only the young know, or can.

But 'age' will soon buy her presence,
- at a cost unknown -
And lost forever, will be that so precious,
That only a young child can ever own.

Bakewell Burt

TRUE LOVE

(Dedicated to my darling wife, Dorothy on the occasion of her passing away, November 11th 1991 - Remembrance Day).

You were the love of my life
My heart, my soul, my all.
Yesterday my darling wife
You took your final call.

Yesterday I held your hand
A touch, a smile, a kiss.
Now I hold your wedding ring
Which bound our wedded bliss.

Now that you have gone my dear
The light of my life has gone.
How can I face the coming years
When yesterday we were as one?

We shared our lives for forty years
I thank you for them all.
Filled with happiness, joy and tears
Together we stood tall.

Now I face my life alone
My grief is hard to bear.
But, our children who are part of you
Will take me in their care.

Then when at last I leave, my love
This life with all its woes.
I'll lie myself beside you
And we'll sleep in sweet repose.

J W Hewing